55 Fantastic Fudges

Gia Scott

ISBN: 1493734598
ISBN-13: 978-1493734597

DEDICATION

For all of my sweet toothed friends, here are enough fudge recipes to ensure you stay in shape (round IS a shape!) and seek false teeth too.

Table of Contents

ACKNOWLEDGMENTS

To Elizabeth Jenkins for her critique as well as the cover photograph.
For my Mom, who is really the family fudge expert.

Fudge—the History

Fudge has been around for some time, over a century now, as a homemade candy. While the exact origins are lost to culinary history, the commonly accepted theory of its origins is that it was a batch of caramels that went "bad", creating the beloved fudge. Since then, it has been improved, adapted, adulterated, modified, vilified, and worshipped, often in the same recipe! Today, we can find everything from flaming hot to exotic in fudge flavors, and a visit to a candy shop specializing in fudge can mean a trip around the world for flavors too.

Creamy and sweet, but even though chocolate is a classic favorite; people enjoy a lot more flavors than merely chocolate. It's a classic homemade candy, and everyone loves it. It makes good gifts; it can brighten anyone's mood too. Nothing is better than homemade fudge!

The ingredients vary, as does the complexity of the recipes. One thing never changes though.

Use the highest quality and freshest ingredients you can to make the best fudge!

Things to Remember

Sweetened condensed milk and evaporated milk are entirely different products and they cannot be substituted for each other because of these differences. Use the type called for in the recipe, or it will not work correctly.

Brown sugar is always packed to measure it.

"Sugar", when unaccompanied by any descriptive term, is simply standard white crystalized sugar. Use cane sugar or beet sugar as you like.

Cream comes in a couple of different grades. "Light" cream is also known as "half and half." Heavy whipping cream is the heavy cream.

Do not substitute margarine for butter. They are not the same, and margarine can cause problems with seizing. Always read the recipe entirely and assemble all ingredients before beginning to make fudge. This prevents errors, as well as discovering (all too late too!) that you are out of an essential ingredient for the fudge or that you have missed or not clearly understood an important step.

For error-proof fudge making, measure all ingredients before starting, placing each one in a container conveniently located near your work area. While this may seem silly and a waste of time, it goes a long ways towards stress-free fudge making, as well as reducing the number of errors that can occur. Always double check quantities as you are measuring to help prevent errors as well.

Use a good candy thermometer, and when using it, make sure that the tip of the thermometer does NOT touch the bottom of the pan. If it does, you will not get an accurate temperature, and your fudge will probably not turn out correctly. Pre-warm the candy thermometer before adding it to hot candy by immersing it in a container of hot water. This prevents damage to the thermometer from the thermal shock of being submerged in the very hot candy.

Be very careful while cooking candy. The hot sugar mixtures will boil and foam profusely on occasion, and can result in severe burns. Candy making is not an activity to engage children in, and it is often best to make sure young children are far away from the stove while making candy too.

It is possible, though not really recommended, to make fudge without a thermometer. Microwave fudges and other fudges that do not require cooking to a particular temperature are the obvious first choices. The cooked old-fashioned fudges can be made using the traditional stages determined by dropping a small amount of the sugar syrup into a bowl of ice water. There is a much larger margin of error in this method, and you are more likely , especially as a novice, to have fudge come out either over or under cooked which will result in hard, crumbly fudge (overcooked) or soft fudge that won't set up properly (undercooked.)

All candies, including fudge, are affected by the current weather conditions. It is not recommended to try making fudge, especially for the novice candy maker, when the humidity is high, as on a rainy day. Cool, dry weather is the most conducive to fudge making success.

Candy making, even fudge, does require developing a skill. Sometimes, you may make an error in judgment, and as a result, the fudge may not set up correctly or may set up before you can get it into the pan. When this happens, the fudge that does not set up correctly can be put in jars and refrigerated or frozen to use as ice cream topping or even a secret filling inside of muffins! The fudge that becomes too hard can be scraped, pried, chiseled, or gouged out of the pan, broken into small pieces, and used as chips in cookies, muffins, cakes, or even in another batch of fudge for an entirely different kind of "rocky road to success" fudge.

Shopping

Most ingredients are available at your local grocery store. However, the gourmet flavorings may be more difficult to obtain. LorAnn's are probably the best, as well as the most familiar to candy makers. This is their website, and they conveniently do mail order.
https://www.lorannoils.com/c-6-super-strength-flavors.aspx

Most grocery stores carry a variety of chocolates for cooking, including Ghirardelli chocolate (my favorite). However, there is also the option of mail order. Here is the Ghirardelli website.
http://www.ghirardelli.com/store/shop-products/collections/baking-products.html/

For those shopping in foreign countries, the one ingredient that seems to confuse and baffle is "marshmallow cream". It IS sold in the UK and Australia. It may be called marshmallow crème or marshmallow fluff as well.

Equipment

It does not take a lot of specialized equipment to make fudge. To make all of these recipes, only a few items are needed.

2 quart microwave safe bowl
8 oz. microwave safe bowl
3 quart heavy saucepan
Candy thermometer
8" square pan
9" square pan
Thin sharp knife
Aluminum foil
Sturdy wooden spoon
Measuring cups
Measuring spoons

Candy Gifts

Giving fudge as a gift is often very appropriate as well as highly appreciated. It's one of the favored gifts for holidays, whether it is a co-worker, neighbor, friend, or as a "Secret Santa." It's also great for housewarmings, hostess gifts and many other occasions because it is impossible to duplicate the artisan effect of delicious homemade fudge in the average factory. Homemade candy says "I care enough to give you something I made myself."

Part of the gift giving process is the packaging. While your gift of homemade fudge will be appreciated even if it is presented on a plastic-wrapped paper plate, a more creative presentation can give your candy more cachet as a gift. This manner of presentation has been known to candy makers throughout the centuries, and professionals have come up with very elaborate boxes for chocolates and other candies. These elaborate (and often antique) candy boxes can give you a number of ideas on presentation as well.

The more artistic and crafty selections include hand decorating (with paint, decals or decoupage) pre-made cardboard or wooden boxes, then lining the box with fancy foil or colored cellophane (food safe, of course!) The individual pieces of fudge are then placed in purchased paper cups inside, or can be individually wrapped in waxed paper or plastic wrap. With a variety of flavors of fudge and the elaborate packaging, it is a gift worthy of giving.

Another option, especially for those with less time or less artistic bent, is to purchase an attractive candy dish or platter, then arrange the fudge on the platter, wrapping the entire arrangement in a shrink wrap bag or plastic wrap. Vintage or antique candy platters, plates, or dishes can also be an option. Wrapping each piece of fudge individually adds a great deal to the effect of a gourmet treat too.

Small labels, either computer printed or hand lettered can be attached to the different flavored fudges. Another alternative is to use colored adhesive dots or stars, color coded (don't forget to include a chart showing your secret code with the platter, just like a box of chocolates with their map of flavors) to indicate the flavor.

Another great packaging idea is the gift basket, whether petite or grand in size. With individually wrapped pieces of fudge or small packages of different flavors, accompanied by cocoa mix (homemade or commercially packaged) or coffee (individual pot-sized gourmet flavors are available at most grocery stores) can be a great start. Adding little extras, perhaps also homemade, such as cookies, fruit, other candies, etc. can become a gorgeous gift as well. Wrapped in shrink wrap, which is easily shrunk over the basket using a standard hand held hair dryer, as well as a ribbon for decoration and a gift card, turns it from a simple gift into one that will impress the most jaded recipient.

Another popular gift giving package is to use purchased tins, arranging the fudge, often with other homemade treats, inside of the tin. This makes for a nice, but still quickly packaged, gift. For smaller sized giving, using inexpensive or novelty coffee mugs as the container is quick, easy, and can be customized to fit the recipient's personality. This is a popular option for co-workers as well.

Don't be afraid to use accessories for your packaging. There are a variety of shredded papers and cellophanes to nestle the packaged fudge into, as well as colored or plain papers to line the container with. Paper cups are also available in a variety of plain and patterns, and the "miniature" cupcake cups also work. Another option for paper cups is to use standard cupcake wrappers and place several pieces of fudges inside each wrapper—a lone 1" square of fudge will appear lost inside of a standard cupcake wrapper!

While the fudge itself is always the star of the gift, the packaging creates the ambience of the overall gift. The more impressive the presentation, the more impressed your recipient will undoubtedly be with your thoughtfulness and effort. It's also a great creative outlet for many people, while others find the challenge of packaging more daunting. Choose a packaging that is appropriate for the recipient, however, and the process becomes much simpler.

Peanut Butter Chocolate Fudge

Everyone has a soft spot for that favorite flavor combination of peanut butter and chocolate! It's absolutely irresistible.

1 14 oz. can sweetened condensed milk
1/2 c. peanut butter
6 oz. milk chocolate chips
6 oz. butterscotch chips
3/4 c. dry roasted peanuts, coarsely chopped
1 tsp. vanilla

In heavy saucepan, heat sweetened condensed milk and peanut butter over medium heat until it just begins to boil while stirring constantly.

Remove from heat. Stir in chocolate and butterscotch chips until smooth. Add peanuts and vanilla.

Spread evenly into wax paper lined 8 or 9" square pan. Cool in refrigerator until firm, about 2 hours. Cut into 1" squares and store in airtight container in refrigerator.

Old Fashioned Peanut Butter Fudge

This is another chocolate and peanut butter combination, this time using cocoa, without the butterscotch addition. Delicious!

3 c. sugar
1 c. evaporated milk
1/4 c. cocoa
1/2 c. peanut butter
1 tbsp. margarine
1 tbsp. butter

Butter 9x9" pan.

In heavy saucepan, combine sugar, evaporated milk, and cocoa. Stir over high heat until mixture comes to a rolling boil. Lower heat to medium and continue cooking to soft ball stage.

Remove from heat. Add peanut butter and margarine. Beat by hand with wooden spoon until creamy. Pour into prepared pan. Allow to cool and cut into 1" squares.

Peanut Butter Chocolate Marble Fudge

This peanut butter and chocolate combination is marbled, creating visual interest along with the flavor combination.

1 14 oz. can sweetened condensed milk
2 c. semi-sweet chocolate chips
2 c. peanut butter chips
2 pinches salt
unsalted butter, softened

Line an 8" square pan with foil, pressing into corners and overhanging sides. Brush the foil with butter.

Combine 3/4 c. sweetened condensed milk, semi-sweet chocolate, and pinch of salt in medium saucepan. Combine remaining sweetened condensed milk, peanut butter chips, and pinch of salt in second saucepan. Put both pans over low heat and cook, stirring occasionally, until chips are melted and smooth.

Spoon the chocolate mixture into prepared pan, leaving spaces between spoonfuls. Spoon peanut butter mixture into gaps. Brush and 8" square of parchment with butter and lay it directly on the fudge, pressing to flatten evenly and fill gaps.

Let cool until firm. Using foil, lift fudge out of pan and cut into 1" squares. Store up to 1 week in airtight container in refrigerator.

Banana Fudge

Banana fudge? Sure!
Imagine a gift box or basket, with individually wrapped squares of fudge of many flavors. This one would surely be a favorite, as well as going so well with chocolate, peanut butter, strawberry…and a host of other flavors.

3 1/2 c. sugar
1/2 tsp. salt
1 c. half & half
3/4 c. butter
3 tbsp. light corn syrup
1 c. mashed ripe banana (about 3 medium)
1 tbsp. vanilla
1/4 c. finely chopped walnuts (optional)

In heavy saucepan, put sugar, salt, half & half, butter, corn syrup and bananas. Over moderate heat, stirring constantly, cook until mixture reaches soft ball (238 degrees F.) Remove from heat.

Cool without stirring until candy temperature reaches 110 degrees (or bottom of pan feels warm to the touch). Add vanilla and nuts. Beat with wooden spoon until candy becomes thick and begins to lose its gloss. Turn into a buttered 8" square pan. Let stand until firm, and then cut into 1" squares.

Chocolate Banana Fudge

It's a creamy version of a chocolate covered frozen banana, all in a tiny 1" square. Almost everyone falls in love with this flavor combination.

1 ripe banana, mashed
2 oz. unsweetened chocolate, chopped
1/2 c. brown sugar
1 1/2 c. sugar
3/4 c. milk
1/8 tsp. salt
2 tbsp. corn syrup
3 tbsp. butter, cut into small pieces
1/2 tsp. vanilla

Prepare an 8" square pan by lining it with foil and spraying with non-stick spray or buttering it evenly.
In medium saucepan, combine sugars, chocolate, milk, salt, corn syrup and banana over medium high heat. Stir constantly until sugar dissolves and mixture looks well combined.

Cook, stirring occasionally, until mixture reaches soft ball stage. (240 degrees F.) Remove from heat, drop butter into fudge but do not stir.

Cool fudge until lukewarm. Add vanilla and stir with wooden spoon until mixture thickens and becomes stiff. Spoon into prepared pan and spread evenly. Allow to sit at room temperature, 2-3 hours, or until set, and then cut into 1" squares.

Sour Cream Fudge

With a hint of the sour from the sour cream, it's a real taste treat, studded with pecans.

3/4 c. sour cream
2 tbsp. butter
2 tbsp. corn syrup
1/4 c. milk
2 c. sugar
1 1/2 tsp. vanilla
2/3 c. chopped pecans

Prepare an 8" square baking pan by lining with foil and spraying with non-stick spray or buttering evenly.

Combine sour cream, sugar, corn syrup, milk, and butter in large saucepan over medium high heat. Stir until sugar is dissolved. Boil mixture, stirring occasionally, until it reaches soft ball stage. (240 degrees F.) Remove from heat.

Allow mixture to cool to lukewarm. Add vanilla and beat with wooden spoon until mixture begins to thicken. Stir in pecans. Pour into prepared pan, spreading evenly. Allow mixture to set at room temperature before cutting into 1" squares.

Chocolate Sour Cream Fudge

This fudge combines the complex flavors of both the chocolate and the sour cream with the sugar and vanilla to make unique fudge filled with flavor.

1 1/2 c. brown sugar
1 1/2 c. sugar
1 1/2 c. sour cream
6 tbsp. light corn syrup
1/4 tsp. salt
3 oz. unsweetened chocolate, finely chopped
1 1/2 tsp. vanilla

Prepare an 8" square pan by lining it with aluminum foil and spraying with nonstick cooking spray or buttering evenly.

Put brown sugar, sugar, corn syrup, and salt in large heavy saucepan over medium heat. Stir until sugar dissolves, then cover the pan and bring to a boil.

When the mixture begins boiling, remove lid and insert candy thermometer. Boil until mixture reaches soft boil (240 degrees F.)

Remove fudge from heat. Sprinkle finely chopped chocolate and vanilla on top, but do not stir. Let fudge cool to 175 degrees F, which should take about 15 minutes. Remove candy thermometer and begin beating the fudge with a wooden spoon until it loses its glossy appearance. (5-15 minutes) As soon as fudge is thickening and is no longer glossy, scrape fudge into prepared pan. Work quickly before fudge sets. Smooth top of fudge and allow to sit at room temperature, about 2 hours.

Once fudge sets, cut into 1" squares to serve. Store at room temperature in airtight container for up to 2 weeks.

Caramel Fudge

A creamy fudge, almost as though it doesn't know whether it was going to be a fudge or a caramel!

1 c. sugar
1/2 c. butter
2 tbsp. light corn syrup
1 14 oz. can sweetened condensed milk

Line an 8" square pan with foil and spray with non-stick spray or butter evenly.

Put sugar, butter, and corn syrup in saucepan. Stir over low heat until dissolved. Add sweetened condensed milk, bring to a boil, and then reduce heat. Stir with a wooden spoon until mixture turns a deep golden caramel color and has thickened.

Pour mixture into prepared pan. Allow to cool completely. Cut into 1" squares. Store in air tight container in refrigerator for up to a week.

Easy Caramel Fudge

This recipe uses white chocolate and miniature marshmallows to ensure it sets up perfectly every time.

2 c. dark brown sugar
1/4 c. butter
3/4 c. evaporated milk
2 c. miniature marshmallows
1 (12 oz.) pkg. white chocolate chips
1 tsp. vanilla
1 c. chopped pecans

Line an 8" square pan with foil. Spray with non-stick spray or coat evenly with butter.

In heavy saucepan, cook brown sugar, butter, and evaporated milk over medium high heat, stirring constantly, until sugar is dissolved. Heat to boiling while still stirring constantly. Reduce heat to low, and boil gently without stirring for 5 minutes. Remove saucepan from heat and stir in marshmallows, white chocolate and vanilla. Stir until ingredients are all melted and evenly mixed into a smooth mixture. Stir in chopped pecans. Quickly spread in pan. Cool in refrigerator until completely cool and set. Cut into 1" squares. Store in air tight container in refrigerator.

Mocha Fudge

The classic combination of coffee and chocolate come together in this mocha fudge.

2 c. sugar
1 c. half and half
1/2 c. brown sugar
1/2 c. cocoa
2 tbsp. instant coffee granules
2 tbsp. light corn syrup
2 tbsp. butter
1/4 tsp. salt
2 tsp. vanilla

Line an 8" square pan with foil. Butter foil.

Butter sides of a heavy saucepan. Place sugar, half and half, brown sugar, cocoa, coffee, corn syrup, butter and salt in pan. Cook, stirring constantly, over medium heat until mixture begins to boil. Put candy thermometer in pan and reduce heat to medium low. Continue boiling until thermometer reaches soft ball stage (240 degrees F.) which takes about 25 minutes.

Remove saucepan from heat. Add vanilla, but do not stir. cool without stirring until mixture reaches 110 degrees F. (Pan is warm on bottom) Remove thermometer and beat mixture with a wooden spoon until candy begins to thicken. Continue beating until candy loses its gloss (5-10 minutes total) Immediately spread fudge evenly in prepared pan. Let cool to room temperature, and remove fudge from pan. Cut into 1" squares.

Store at room temperature for up to a week.

Coffee Fudge

It's like the perfect rich, creamy cup of coffee, laced with cream and sugar to perfection, only to melt on your tongue in an explosion of flavors.

3 c. sugar
1 1/2 c. half and half
3 tbsp. light corn syrup
2 tbsp. instant coffee
dash of salt
2 tbsp. butter
1 tsp. vanilla

Line 8" square pan with foil and butter foil or coat with non-stick spray.

Butter large heavy saucepan and add sugar, half and half, corn syrup, instant coffee, and salt. Stir constantly over medium high heat until mixture reaches a boil. Reduce heat to medium low and boil without stirring to thread stage (234 degrees F.) Remove from heat and add butter and vanilla. Do not stir! Cool mixture to 110 degrees F (pan will be warm on bottom) Pour into prepared pan. Cool at room temperature. When completely cool, cut into 1" squares.

Cinnamon Roll Fudge

Sometimes, it's hard to imagine something, but then once you try it, you can't imagine it NOT going together. That's this fudge. It's like a candied cinnamon roll!

3 c. sugar
3/4 c. butter
2/3 c. evaporated milk
10 oz. cinnamon chips
7 oz. marshmallow cream
2 tsp. vanilla
1/2 tsp. salt
1 tsp. cinnamon
3/4 c. toasted pecans, chopped coarsely
1/2 c. powdered sugar
2 1/4 tsp. milk
1/4 tsp. vanilla

Prepare a 9" square pan by lining with foil and spraying with non-stick spray or buttering evenly.

Put sugar, evaporated milk and butter in large pan over medium heat. Stir constantly until butter and sugar dissolve. Continue to cook, stirring frequently, until mixture starts to boil. Keep candy at rolling boil, stirring constantly, for five minutes. Remove from heat, stir in cinnamon chips and continue stirring until chips are melted and mixture is smooth.

Stir in marshmallow cream, vanilla, cinnamon, salt, and pecans. Once mixture is smooth and evenly mixed, pour fudge into prepared pan and smooth into even layer. Allow to set at room temperature for several hours.

After fudge is set and cooled, make glaze by combining powdered sugar, milk and vanilla. Put glaze into small zip close bag, and snip off tiny corner. Drizzle in a crisscross pattern over the fudge and allow to set for at least 15 minutes.

When glaze has set, remove fudge from pan and cut into 1" squares. Fudge can be stored at room temperature or in refrigerator in air tight container for up to 2 weeks.

Peaches and Cream Fudge

Peaches and cream are another Southern favorite, and go with summer like swimming and beaches do. Putting them together with fudge turns them into an instant delight.

2/3 c. evaporated milk
2 1/2 c. sugar
3/4 c. peach puree
7 oz. marshmallow cream
2 tbsp. butter
6 oz. white chocolate chips
1 tsp. vanilla

Line a 9" pan with foil. Spray with non-stick spray or butter evenly.

In large heavy saucepan, heat milk and sugar over medium heat. Bring to a boil, stirring occasionally with a wooden spoon. Mix in peach puree, and then return mixture to a boil. Stir in marshmallow cream and butter. Bring to a rolling boil, stirring occasionally, for 18-20 minutes.

Remove from heat. Add chips and vanilla and stir. Pour into pan, smoothing top if necessary.

When completely cool, remove from pan and cut into 1" squares. Store in airtight container in refrigerator.

Apple Pie Fudge

If you have never had it, you've likely never imagined it either. Once you've had it, you'll wonder how you ever lived without it!

1 c. applesauce
3/4 c. butter
2/3 c. evaporated milk
3 c. sugar
2 c. marshmallow cream
1 tsp. vanilla
1 c. white chocolate chips
1 tsp. cinnamon
1/2 tsp. nutmeg

Line 8" pan with foil, coat with non-stick spray or butter evenly.

Mix applesauce, butter, milk, and sugar in large heavy saucepan. Over medium high heat, while stirring constantly, bring to a boil Remove from heat and add marshmallow cream, vanilla, white chocolate, cinnamon and nutmeg. Stir to blend well. Pour into prepared pan.

Allow to cool completely. Cut into 1" squares.

Caramel Apple Fudge

Caramel apples on a stick are admittedly messy, as well as being a rather large serving to commit yourself to. It's so much easier when that wonderful creamy/sweet/juicy/sticky flavor is combined into a delicate 1" square of perfect candy.

1 c. applesauce
3/4 c. butter
2/3 c. evaporated milk
3 c. sugar
2 c. marshmallow cream
1 tsp. vanilla
2 c. powdered sugar
1 12 oz. pkg. caramel bits

Line 9" pan with foil, coat with non-stick spray or butter evenly.

Mix applesauce, butter, milk, and sugar in large heavy saucepan. Over medium high heat, while stirring constantly, bring to a boil. Remove from heat and add marshmallow cream, vanilla, and powdered sugar. Stir to blend well. Quickly and gently add caramel bits. Pour into prepared pan.

Allow to cool completely. Cut into 1" squares.

Key Lime Fudge

Key lime juice, combined with macadamia nuts, rendered into a creamy and delicious fudge and it's a perfect combination.

3 c. white chocolate chips
1 14 oz. can sweetened condensed milk
2 tsp. finely grated lime peel
2 tbsp. key or regular lime juice
1 c. coarsely chopped macadamia nuts
few drops green food coloring

Line 8" square pan with foil. Butter or coat foil with non-stick spray.

In a large heavy saucepan, stir milk and white chocolate together over low heat, until mixture is smooth and white chocolate is melted. Stir in lime peel and lime juice with food coloring to make a pale green. Add macadamia nuts.

Spread mixture evenly in prepared pan. Cover and chill for 2 hours or until firm.

Remove fudge from pan. Cut into 1" squares. Store in air tight container at room temperature for up to a week.

Orange Dreamsicle Fudge

Creamy and dreamy, orange swirled with white, it's beautiful, colorful, unmistakable, and delicious too. You won't want to NOT offer this in your repertoire.

3/4 c. butter
2 c. sugar
3/4 c. heavy whipping cream
1 (12 oz.) pkg. white chocolate chips
1 (7 oz.) jar marshmallow cream
1 tbsp. orange extract
orange food coloring

Prepare a 9x13" pan by lining with foil and coating with non-stick spray or buttering evenly.

In large heavy saucepan, combine sugar, cream and butter over medium heat, stirring continually. Cook until butter melts and sugar is dissolved. Brush down sides of pan with wet pastry brush to eliminate crystals.

Bring the mixture to a boil, stirring constantly. Once mixture is boiling, insert candy thermometer. Cook candy, without stirring, until it reachs 240 degrees (soft ball), normally about 4-5 minutes.

Remove from heat and quickly stir in marshmallow cream and white chocolate. Stir until white chocolate is completely melted and mixture is smooth.

Working very quickly, pour about one third of fudge mixture into bowl and set aside. To remaining fudge, add orange extract and orange food coloring, stirring until it is a smooth, even color. Pour into prepared pan and smooth to make an even layer.

Drop white fudge by spoonfuls into orange fudge, and then, using a toothpick or knife, swirl white through the orange fudge. Coat a 9x13" piece of foil with non-stick spray and press down on top of fudge to smooth out swirls.

Allow to set at room temperature for 2 hours. To cut, remove from pan, and use a very sharp thin knife to cut into 1" squares. Store in airtight container in refrigerator for up to a week, bringing to room temperature to serve.

Easy Dark Chocolate Orange Fudge

The combination of dark chocolate and oranges always reminds me of Christmas, but it is delicious any time of the year.

2 1/2 c. Hershey's Special Dark Chocolate Chips
1 can (14 oz.) sweetened condensed milk
1 tsp. grated orange zest
1/2 tsp. orange extract

Prepare 8" square pan by lining with foil and spraying with non-stick spray or buttering evenly.

In heavy saucepan, over low heat, stirring constantly with wooden spoon, heat milk until very hot. Remove from heat, stir in chocolate chips and mix until chocolate is evenly distributed and melted. Add orange zest and orange extract. Pour into prepared pan.

Let cool at room temperature. When completely cool, cut into 1" squares. Store in refrigerator in air tight container for up to two weeks.

Pumpkin Fudge

Pumpkin fudge is excellent as a fall choice, tempting at those bake sales too. It's also an easy option to carry to work, church, or club meetings for a sweet treat.

2 c. sugar
1 c. brown sugar
3/4 c. butter
2/3 c. evaporated milk
1/2 c. canned pumpkin
1 tsp. cinnamon
1/4 tsp. nutmeg
1/2 tsp. allspice
1 tsp. ginger
1 (12 oz.) pkg. white chocolate chips
1 (7 oz.) jar marshmallow cream
1 c. chopped pecans
1 1/2 tsp. vanilla

Prepare 9x13" pan by lining with foil and spraying with non-stick spray or buttering evenly.

In heavy saucepan, combine sugar, brown sugar, butter, milk, pumpkin, cinnamon, nutmeg, allspice, and ginger. Heat over medium heat until sugar dissolves, stirring constantly. Continue heating until mixture reaches a boil, stirring constantly. Cook until mixture reaches softball stage (240 degrees F.)

Remove pan from heat. Stir in white chocolate chips and stir until chocolate is melted and mixture is evenly mixed. Add marshmallow cream, pecans, and vanilla, stirring to combine well. Pour into prepared pan and cool to room temperature.

Cut fudge into 1" squares. Store in air tight container in refrigerator.

Easy Eggnog Fudge

What says winter holidays better than eggnog? It's the perfect choice to serve as an alternative to the traditional chocolate fudges and the spicy slabs of gingerbread too.

2 c. sugar
1/2 c. butter
3/4 c. heavy cream OR eggnog
1 (12 oz.) pkg. white chocolate chips
1/2 tsp. nutmeg
7 oz. jar marshmallow cream
1 tsp. rum extract
1/2 tsp. vanilla
1-2 drops yellow food coloring
additional nutmeg for sprinkling

Line a 9" square pan with foil. Coat foil with non-stick spray or butter evenly.

Combine sugar, butter, and eggnog into heavy saucepan. Bring to a boil over medium heat. Once boiling, insert candy thermometer and reduce heat to medium low, and cook until thermometer reaches 234 degrees (soft ball) while stirring constantly.

Remove from heat and add white chocolate, stirring until chips melt and mixture is smooth. Add food coloring to make a slightly creamy colored mixture (not too much!). Add marshmallow cream, nutmeg, rum extract and vanilla and mix until combined well.

Pour into prepared pan and sprinkle with nutmeg. Allow

to cool at room temperature. When completely cool, cut into 1" squares.

Pomegranate Fudge

Bright maroon-red, the unusual flavor of pomegranates give this fudge a real kick. It also stands out in the crowd, perfect for platters or gift boxes.

3 c. sugar
1/2 c. pomegranate juice (make sure it's pure pomegranate juice)
1/3 c. heavy whipping cream
3/4 c. butter
2 1/2 c. white chocolate chips
1/2 tsp. pomegranate flavoring
7 oz. marshmallow cream
red & blue food coloring

Line a 9" square pan with foil. Coat with non-stick spray or butter evenly.

Combine sugar, butter, pomegranate juice and cream into a heavy saucepan. Heat until boiling over medium heat, stirring constantly. When boiling, insert candy thermometer and reduce heat to medium low, cook, stirring constantly, to soft boil (234 degrees F.)

Remove from heat. With wooden spoon, stir in chocolate chips until melted and smooth. Add flavoring, marshmallow cream, and food coloring to make a light pink mixture.

Pour mixture into prepared pan; allow to cool at room

temperature for several hours. When firm, cut into 1" squares.

Fresh Blueberry Fudge

This uses fresh berries, and has an almost cheesecake-like flavor too.

1 (8 oz.) pkg. cream cheese
1/4 tsp. lemon flavor
1/4 tsp. salt
1 (12 oz.) pkg. white chocolate chips, melted & cooled
3 c. sifted powdered sugar
1 1/4 c. toasted slivered almonds
1 c. fresh blueberries

Line 8" square pan with foil.

In bowl, beat cream cheese, lemon flavor, and salt until smooth. Beat in white chocolate. On medium low speed, add powdered sugar, 1 c. at a time. Increase speed to high and beat for 2 minutes. Fold in nuts and blueberries.

Spread mixture into prepared pan. Cover and refrigerate 8 hours or overnight. Turn fudge out onto work surface and carefully peel off foil. Turn fudge right side up and cut into 1" squares. Keep refrigerated and serve cold. Keeps up to a week in refrigerator when tightly wrapped.

Blueberry Fudge

Using dried blueberries and boosting the flavor with blueberry flavoring, these are entirely different from the fresh blueberry version.

3 c. sugar
3/4 c. butter
2/3 c. evaporated milk
1/2 c. frozen blueberries, thawed
1 (12 oz.) pkg. white chocolate chips
1 (7 oz.) jar marshmallow cream
1 c. chopped pecans (optional)
1 c. coarsely chopped dried blueberries
1 tsp. vanilla
1/2 tsp. blueberry flavoring
few drops blue food coloring

Prepare 9x13" pan by lining with foil and spraying with non-stick spray or buttering evenly.

In heavy saucepan, combine sugar, butter, milk, and frozen blueberries. Heat over medium heat until sugar dissolves, stirring constantly. Continue heating until mixture reaches a boil, stirring constantly. Cook until mixture reaches softball stage (240 degrees F.)

Remove pan from heat. Stir in white chocolate chips and stir until chocolate is melted and mixture is evenly mixed. Add marshmallow cream, pecans, dried blueberries, blueberry flavoring, and vanilla, stirring to combine well. Add blue food coloring by the drop and stir to achieve a pale blue color. Pour into prepared pan and cool to room temperature.

Cut fudge into 1" squares. Store in air tight container in refrigerator.

Hellishly Hot Habanero Fudge

This is a much hotter, more exotic flavor than most of us are inclined to eat. Even so, for those who love the hot, there is plenty to love here with this novelty fudge.

4 habanero peppers, finely minced
8 oz. marshmallow cream
3 c. milk chocolate chips
1 1/2 c. sugar
2/3 c. evaporated milk
1/4 c. butter
1 tsp. vanilla
pinch of salt

Prepare 8" square pan by lining with foil and spraying with non-stick spray or evenly buttering.

Place marshmallow cream, sugar, evaporated milk, butter, and salt in heavy saucepan over medium heat. Stirring constantly, bring to a boil and cook for 5 minutes. Remove from heat and add chocolate chips, minced peppers, and vanilla. Stir until melted and uniform. Pour into prepared pan.

Chill in refrigerator until firm, about 3 hours. Remove from pan, cut into 1" squares. Store in air tight container in refrigerator for up to a week.

Southwestern Fudge

Chocolate was a food from the Aztecs and Mayans, and has a long history of being combined with many things, including chilis. The pine nuts combine well with the chili powder, and sprinkled with salt, it's a grown up sweet with a distinctly southwestern flavor.

3 c. semi-sweet chocolate chips
1 c. toasted pine nuts
2 tbsp. New Mexico red chili powder (hot or mild, according to taste)
1 (14 oz.) sweetened condensed milk
1 tsp. vanilla
1 tbsp. coarse or flaked salt

Prepare 9" square pan by lining with foil and spraying with non-stick spray or coating evenly with butter.

Heat sweetened condensed milk in glass bowl in microwave until very hot but not boiling. Add chocolate chips and stir until melted. Stir in chili powder, toasted pine nuts, and vanilla until evenly mixed. Pour mixture into prepared pan. Sprinkle with salt, pressing lightly with piece of foil coated with non-stick spray to ensure salt adheres. Do not press INTO the fudge, but rather just enough to make sure salt sticks to fudge.

Cool in refrigerator until hardened, about 2 hours. Using sharp thin knife, cut into 1" squares. Store in single layer in air tight container in refrigerator. Bring to room temperature to serve.

Velveeta Fudge

Velveeta fudge may be one of the strangest inventions, but it's also a classic. It's also a huge surprise to realize that when the fudge is made, the cheese flavor is really not there.

1 c. butter, softened
8 oz. Velveeta cheese
1 1/2 pounds (about 5 c.) unsifted powdered sugar
1/2 c. cocoa
1/2 c. non-fat dry milk
2 tsp. vanilla
2 c. coarsely chopped pecans

Prepare 9" square pan by lining with foil and spraying with non-stick spray or buttering evenly.

In large saucepan, heat butter and cheese together over medium heat, stirring often. Remove from heat. Sift powdered sugar and cocoa together. Add powdered sugar mixture to cheese mixture, mixing well. Stir in non-fat dry milk, vanilla, and nuts. Turn into prepared pan. Chill until firm and then cut into 1" squares with thin sharp knife.

Store in refrigerator in airtight container for up to a week.

Gourmet Smoked Bacon Fudge

Bacon, chocolate, sweet…what isn't there to love?

It's also very modern—bacon and chocolate may be a fairly recent pairing, in terms of their public social connection, but it's also a delicious pairing!

1/2 c. dark cocoa powder
2 c. white sugar
1/4 tsp. salt
1 tbsp. light corn syrup
1 c. milk
1 tbsp. vanilla
2 tbsp. butter (divided)
2 lbs. smoked bacon, cooked until crisp, well drained, and crumbled (divided)

Prepare 9" square pan by lining with foil and spraying foil with non-stick spray or evenly buttering.

Butter sides of a medium saucepan, and then stir together cocoa, sugar, and salt in pan. Mix in corn syrup and milk until mixture is smooth. Add 1 tbsp. butter and heat over medium heat, stirring constantly, until boiling. Continue to cook to 240 degrees F. (Soft ball stage) without stirring. Remove from heat.

Let mixture cool until bottom of pan feels warm. Stir in vanilla and half of bacon. Pour into prepared 9" pan. Beat with wooden spoon until mixture is thick and begins losing its gloss. Sprinkle remaining bacon on top, pressing lightly to adhere bacon to fudge. Let cool until set.

Cut fudge in 1" squares. Refrigerate in air tight container in refrigerator for up to a week.

Black Walnut Maple Cream Fudge

This is the stuff of dreams, combining two All-American foods, the intensely flavored black walnut with the delicious maple, in this creamy fudge. It's to die for, and a certain favorite among the more classical sweet flavor crowd.

2 c. maple syrup (The real stuff!)
1 tbsp. light corn syrup
3/4 c. heavy whipping cream
1/2 c. chopped black walnuts
butter for pan

Line 9x5" square pan loaf with foil. Coat foil with non-stick spray or butter evenly.

Butter sides of sauce pan. Clip on candy thermometer so that tip is NOT touching the bottom. Add maple syrup, corn syrup, and heavy whipping cream. Heat over medium heat, stirring constantly, until mixture begins to boil. Continue cooking, without stirring, until mixture reaches 240 degrees F. (soft ball stage). Remove from heat.

Remove from heat. Allow to cool in pot until lukewarm (about 120 degrees F.) It will take 30 min to an hour. When cool, add nuts and butter. Beat with mixer until mixture begins to thicken and lose its gloss. Scrape mixture into prepared pan, pressing down firmly with wooden spoon. Let cool completely and remove from pan. Cut into 1" squares.

Store in tightly sealed container up to two weeks at room temperature.

German Chocolate Fudge

A German Chocolate Cake, while having never been to Germany (it's named for the maker of the chocolate used, rather than the country!) combines the classic flavors of chocolate, pecans, coconut and vanilla into a small square of absolute delight. Anyone who loves these flavors will definitely appreciate this fudge.

4 oz. German baking chocolate, chopped
1 (14 oz.) can sweetened condensed milk
1 c. pecans, toasted & finely chopped
1 c. flaked coconut, toasted lightly
2 tsp. vanilla

Prepare 8" square pan by lining with foil and coating foil with non-stick spray or evenly buttering it.

In large glass bowl, combine chocolate and milk. Heat in microwave in 30 second intervals, stirring after each interval, until chocolate is melted and mixture is smooth. Stir in remaining ingredients. Spread in prepared pan. Cover tightly and chill two hours or until firm. Remove from pan and cut into 1" squares. Store up to two weeks in refrigerator in air tight container.

Easy Piña Colada Fudge

The piña colada may have started out as a cocktail, but it's come a long ways since then. The flavor of pineapple, coconut, macadamia nuts, and rum come together to create a tropical flavored delightful sweet that almost conjures up the sea breezes and sandy beaches right in your mouth.

Toast the coconut by spreading it on an ungreased baking sheet and putting it into the oven with the broiler on, leaving the door open for constant vigilance to prevent scorching. Toast it just until it barely shows a hint of brown or tan, and remove from the oven.

To toast the macadamia nuts, spread them on a cookie sheet, just like the coconut was, but do not try to toast them at the same time—they toast at different rates and it does not work. Toasting the nuts whole may be easier than toasting the chopped nuts, but the choice is up to you. Never leave toasting nuts or coconut alone—it's a known Murphy's Law that it will ALWAYS scorch, ruining the ingredient for cooking, as well as causing a definite "aromatherapy problem" for the entire house! Always, the goal is for delicate toasting to bring out the flavor, not to roast them long enough for scorching or even darker shades of tan. Burned nuts are not an attractive flavor.

2 c. white chocolate chips

1 (3.25 oz.) jar macadamia nuts, chopped & toasted, divided

1 (16 oz.) can Vanilla frosting

1/2 c. chopped dried pineapple

1/2 c. toasted flaked coconut

1 tsp. rum extract

1/2 tsp. coconut extract
1/2 tsp. pineapple flavoring

Reserve ¼ c. nuts for garnish and set aside.

Prepare 8" square pan by lining with foil, extending over edges for easy removal. Lightly spray foil with non-stick spray.

In microwave safe bowl, microwave white chocolate chips in 15 second intervals until melted and smooth, stirring between each interval.

Add remaining ingredients to melted chips. Mix well and spread in prepared fan. Sprinkle with reserved nuts. Refrigerate until firm, 1-2 hours.

Lift fudge out of pan by foil. Peel foil away from fudge and cut fudge into 1" squares.

Pistachio Fudge

Pistachios are delicious, and they combine very well to make delicious flavored pale green fudge, great for creating visual contrast when displayed with other fudge flavors.

3/4 c. evaporated milk
2 1/2 c. sugar
1/2 c. butter
2 c. marshmallow cream
8 oz. vanilla flavored candy coating, chopped
1 c. chopped pistachios
1 tsp. vanilla
1 drop green food coloring

Prepare 9x13" pan by lining with foil and spraying with non-stick spray or evenly buttering foil.

In medium sauce pan over medium high heat, combine evaporated milk, sugar, and butter. Bring to a boil, stirring constantly. Without stirring, maintain the boil for 4 minutes. Remove from heat. Stir in marshmallow cream and candy coating. When mixture is smooth and evenly combined, then stir in pistachios and vanilla. Add food coloring, adding more drops as necessary, one drop at a time, to achieve desired shade of pale green. Pour mixture into prepared pan and cool completely. Remove from pan and cut into 1" squares. Stores up to two weeks at room temperature.

Cashew Fudge

Anyone who loves cashews is sure to love this fudge. Chock full of nuts, it is a nut lover's delight.

2 c. sugar
1/3 c. heavy whipping cream
1/2 c. milk
1/8 tsp. coarse kosher salt
1 tsp. vanilla
1 c. cashew butter, at room temperature
1/2 c. fancy whole cashews
1/2 c. chopped cashews

Prepare 8" square pan by lining with well-buttered foil.

In a medium saucepan, combine sugar, cream, milk, and salt. Cook over medium heat, stirring constantly until mixture comes to a boil. Continue cooking, stirring frequently, until it reaches soft ball stage (240 degrees F.)

Remove pan from heat. Stir in vanilla and cashew butter. Continue stirring mixture about 5 minutes, or until the cashew butter is completely combined and the mixture is smooth, thick and lump free. Stir in chopped cashews.

Spread fudge mixture evenly into prepared pan, smoothing top with spatula. Sprinkle whole cashews into top of fudge, pressing lightly. Set aside to cool at room temperature, 1-2 hours.

When fudge is firm and cool, remove from pan and cut into 1" squares with thin sharp knife. Store in air tight container for up to a month.

Butter Pecan Fudge

What could be more Southern than butter pecans? It makes delicious fudge too!

1/2 c. butter
1/2 c. sugar
1/2 c. brown sugar
1/2 c. heavy whipping cream
1/8 tsp. salt
1 tsp. vanilla
2 c. powdered sugar
1 c. pecans, toasted & coarsely chopped

Prepare an 8" square pan by lining with buttered foil (or foil sprayed with non-stick spray).

Combine butter, sugar, brown sugar, cream and salt in a large heavy saucepan. Over medium heat, bring to a boil while stirring often. Stirring constantly, boil for 5 minutes. Remove from heat and stir in vanilla.

Beat in powdered sugar until mixture is smooth. Fold in pecans. Spread into prepared pan and cool to room temperature.

When cool and firm, cut into 1" squares. Store in refrigerator in air tight container for up to two weeks.

Ice Cream Chocolate Fudge

This recipe only has two ingredients so it is critical to have good quality ones. Cheap chocolate and cheap ice cream will result in rather bland fudge. By using ice cream, most of the measuring and mixing has already been done.

24 oz. semi-sweet chocolate chips
1 1/2 c. chocolate ice cream, softened slightly

Prepare an 8" square pan by lining with foil and spraying with non-stick spray or buttering foil evenly.

Place the chocolate chips in microwave safe bowl and microwave in 20 second intervals, stirring after each interval. When chips are nearly melted, remove from microwave and continue stirring until mixture is smooth and creamy. (It should just be warm, not hot.) Add ice cream to chocolate, stirring constantly as it is added. Mixture may get chunky, but that is fine. When ice cream and chocolate are combined, return mixture to microwave for 30 seconds. Stir well. Mixture should be smooth, but if it is not, return to microwave and repeat for 15 seconds, stirring after each interval. Do not heat more than necessary to get a smooth and creamy mixture.

Put mixture into prepared pan. Let cool at room temperature for about 4 hours, or until completely firm. Remove from pan by lifting out foil. Cut fudge into 1" squares. May be stored for up to 2 weeks at room temperature.

Christmas Fudge

The candied fruit, mixed through the white fudge, makes festive fudge that brings out some of the traditional flavors of the winter holidays.

24 oz. (2 bags) white chocolate chips
1 (14 oz.) can sweetened condensed milk
1 tsp. vanilla
pinch of salt
1 c. coarsely chopped candied fruit

Prepare 8" square pan by lining with foil and spraying with non-stick spray or lightly buttering foil.

In heavy saucepan, over low heat, melt chips, condensed milk, vanilla, and salt, while stirring constantly. When mixture is smooth, remove from heat. Stir in candied fruit. Spread evenly in prepared pan and chill for 2 hours or until firm.

Cut into 1" squares. Store in air tight container in refrigerator for up to two weeks.

Vegan Chocolate Fudge

For the vegans in your life, there is also a vegan fudge, tasty enough to win over some non-vegan taste buds too!

6 tbsp. vegan margarine
3 1/2 c. powdered sugar
1/2 c. cocoa
1 tsp. vanilla
1/4 c. soy milk
1 c. chopped nuts (optional)

Prepare a 5x9" loaf pan by lining with foil and lightly coating foil with some vegan margarine.

Place remaining margarine, sugar, cocoa, vanilla and soy milk in a microwave safe bowl. Heat in microwave in 30 second intervals, stirring after each interval, until hot. Stir until smooth and creamy. Add nuts, if desired. Pour mixture into prepared pan. Chill until cold. Remove fudge from pan and cut into 1" squares.

Almond Joy Fudge

While it doesn't contain the candy bars, it does have that amazing flavor punch that comes from combining the chewy texture of the coconut with the joyful crunch of the almonds, as well as the rich chocolate flavor.

3 c. semi-sweet chocolate chips
1 (14 oz.) can sweetened condensed milk
1/4 c. butter
1 c. almonds, coarsely chopped
2 1/3 c. shredded coconut, divided

Prepare 8" square pan by lining with foil and spraying with non-stick spray. Reserve 1/3 c. coconut for garnish, and set aside.

In large microwave safe bowl, combine chocolate chips, milk, and butter. Microwave mixture for 1 minute intervals until melted, stirring after each interval. Stir until candy is smooth and mixed well. Add almonds and all but 1/3 c. coconut. Stir until mixed evenly. Pour fudge into prepared pan and smooth into an even layer. Sprinkle remaining 1/3 c. coconut on top and press lightly to adhere it to the fudge. Place in refrigerator for 2 hours or until cold and firm. Remove from pan and cut into 1" squares. Serve at room temperature. Fudge may be stored in an air tight container in refrigerator for up to two weeks.

Sweet Potato Fudge

Sweet potatoes are a Southern favorite, and it's only natural that they appear in fudge too. They pair well with the sweetness of the milk and white chocolate, accented by the vanilla and spices. It's got enough punch to accompany the fanciest fudges in gift packages and platters, and all of the character of any Southern gentleman.

1 c. white chocolate chips
1/4 c. butter
1 (14 oz.) can sweetened condensed milk
3/4 c. mashed sweet potato
1 tsp. vanilla
3/4 tsp. cinnamon
1/2 tsp. allspice
1/4 tsp. nutmeg
8 c. powdered sugar
2 c. pecans, toasted & chopped

Prepare 8" pan by lining with waxed paper.

In large bowl, melt white chocolate, butter, and milk together in 15 second intervals in the microwave, stirring after each interval, until mixture is smooth and creamy. Pour into mixing bowl and stir in mashed sweet potato, vanilla, cinnamon, allspice, nutmeg, salt, and half of the powdered sugar. Mix with mixer on low speed, scraping bowl to ensure everything is evenly combined. With the machine on, add remaining powdered sugar, 1/2 c. at a time, until it is all incorporated and mixture is very thick. Pour in nuts, stir by hand to mix them evenly, and pour mixture into prepared pan. Smooth top.

Refrigerate mixture until fudge has hardened, about 2 hours. Remove fudge from pan and cut into 1" squares.

Store in refrigerator for up to a week in air tight container.

Traditional Rocky Road Fudge

Rocky Road fudge, with the miniature marshmallows and nuts, is about as traditional as anything could be, regarding candies To keep the marshmallows distinct, they are frozen while the fudge is cooking so that they don't melt when the fudge is poured over them. I don't know who or how this combination was invented, but it's a combination that everyone loves.

2 c. sugar
3/4 c. evaporated milk
2 oz. unsweetened baking chocolate
1 tbsp. light corn syrup
2 tbsp. butter
1 tsp. vanilla
1/2 c. miniature marshmallows, frozen
1/2 c. chopped pecans or walnuts

Prepare 9x5" loaf pan by lining with foil and buttering foil. Sprinkle marshmallows over bottom of the pan, and place pan in freezer while making fudge. (Important!)

Lightly butter inside of 2 quart saucepan. Add sugar, milk, chocolate and corn syrup. Cook over medium high heat until mixture begins to boil. Continue to boil gently, stirring frequently, until mixture reaches 235 degrees F. (soft ball stage) Remove saucepan from heat. Add butter and vanilla to pan but do not stir.

Let mixture cool for about 30 minutes or until just warm when the bottom of the pan is touched. Beat with a wooden spoon until the fudge just begins to thicken. Add chopped nuts, and beat for a few more minutes, until it just begins to lose its gloss but is still pourable. Pour over marshmallows. Let stand until set and cool. Lift fudge out by the foil, and cut into 1" squares. Store in air tight container for up to two weeks.

Almond Cherry Fudge

This is easy microwave fudge. It's also both a pretty and a delicious one, with the pale white fudge accented by the dark dried cherries and the bright red candied cherries, as well as the slivers of almonds scattered throughout.

2 c. (12 oz.) white chocolate chips
1 (14 oz.) can sweetened condensed milk
1/2 c. slivered almonds
1/2 c. red candied cherries, coarsely chopped
1/2 c. dried cherries, coarsely chopped
1 tsp. almond extract

Prepare a 9" square pan by lining with foil and lightly buttering (or spraying with non-stick spray.)

In microwave safe bowl, melt white chocolate and milk on high for 1 minute and stir. Continue microwaving in 15 second intervals, stirring after each interval, until chocolate is melted and mixture is smooth. Stir in almonds, candied cherries, dried cherries, and almond extract. Spread mixture into prepared pan. Cover and chill for 2 hours or until firm.

Using foil, lift fudge out of pan. Cut into 1" squares. Store in air tight container in refrigerator for up to 2 weeks.

Dark Chocolate Cherry Fudge

Dark, creamy and intense chocolate, combined with the chewy flavor of the cherries is always a favorite fudge combination. It contrasts well with other fudges as well, making it a popular choice for gift boxes as well as platters.

1 1/2 c. sugar
2/3 c. evaporated milk
2 tbsp. butter
1/4 tsp. salt
2 c. miniature marshmallows
1 2/3 c. dark chocolate chips
3/4 c. dried cherries, chopped
1 tsp. vanilla extract
1/4 tsp. almond extract (optional)

Prepare 8" square pan by lining with foil.

Combine sugar, milk, butter, and salt in heavy saucepan. Bring to a full rolling boil over medium heat while stirring constantly. Cook, stirring constantly, for 5 minutes. Remove from heat.

Stir in marshmallows, chocolate chips, dried cherries, vanilla, and almond extract. Beat vigorously with wooden spoon until marshmallows are melted and mixture is smooth. Pour into prepared pan. Refrigerate for 2 hours or until cold and firm.. Remove from pan, using foil to lift. Cut into 1" squares.

Store in refrigerator for up to two weeks in air tight container.

Mashed Potato Fudge

Cooks are inventive, as a whole, and often use familiar and common ingredients to "stretch" more expensive ones. Mashed potatoes are often featured in this manner, which is the role they play in this recipe.

1/2 c. cooked potatoes, mashed
2 tbsp. butter
1 lb. powdered sugar
3 squares unsweetened baking chocolate, melted
1 tsp. vanilla
dash of salt

Line 8" square pan with foil, coat with non-stick spray or butter evenly.

Put mashed potatoes into mixing bowl. Add butter and beat. Add powdered sugar and mix well. Add vanilla to melted chocolate, then add with salt to potato mixture. Beat until well mixed.

Spread mixture in prepared pan. Chill until firm. Cut into 1" squares. Store in refrigerator in air tight container for up to a week.

Candy Cane Fudge

Peppermint candy canes and Christmas are kissing cousins, it seems. This fudge, with its bright peppermint flavor and creamy texture, is a perfect reflection of that relationship. It's also pretty!

For the crushed candy, using the round disks rather than the candy canes will result in more "crumble" and less candy cane "dust", ideal for this particular candy's garnish.

20 oz. white chocolate chips (2 bags)
1 (14 oz.) can sweetened condensed milk
1/2 tsp. peppermint extract
1 1/2 c. crushed peppermint candies
paste red food coloring

Line 8" square pan with foil. Spray foil with non-stick cooking spray or evenly butter.

Combine white chocolate chips and sweetened condensed milk in heavy saucepan over medium heat. Stir frequently until chocolate is almost melted. Remove from heat. Stir until smooth and creamy. Stir in peppermint extract and 3/4 c. peppermint pieces. Pour evenly into pan. Using toothpick, pick up a dab of paste red food coloring and swirl toothpick randomly through fudge. When satisfied with color (you do have to work quickly) sprinkle remaining 3/4 c. peppermint candy pieces on top of fudge and press lightly into fudge.

Chill for 2 hours or until cold and firm. Remove from pan and cut into 1" squares.

Crème de Menthe Fudge

Chocolate and mint come together, swirled with green and brown, and cool creaminess throughout. It's beautiful as well as delicious.

2 1/2 c. sugar
3/4 tsp. salt
1/4 c. butter
3/4 c. evaporated milk
1 (7 1/2 oz.) marshmallow cream
1 (12 oz.) pkg. dark chocolate chips
1/2 c. white chocolate chips
3/4 tsp. vanilla
1 tsp. peppermint extract
1/4 tsp. spearmint extract
2-3 drops green food coloring

Line 9" square pan with foil. Spray foil with non-stick spray or butter evenly.

In heavy skillet, heat sugar, salt, butter, milk, and marshmallow cream over low heat, stirring constantly, until blended. Continue heating to a full rolling boil.

Boil slowly for five minutes, stirring constantly. Remove from heat. Stir in vanilla, peppermint, and spearmint. Separate about 1/4 of mixture into bowl and add white chocolate to bowl. Stir dark chocolate into remaining mixture in pan. Stir dark chocolate mixture until smooth and creamy. Pour into prepared pan.

Working quickly, add 2 drops of green food coloring to mixture in bowl and stir until creamy and smooth, adding 1 or 2 drops of food coloring to get desired shade. Drop green mixture into dark chocolate mixture by spoonful and swirl with thin knife to marble mixture. If necessary, press sheet of foil sprayed with non-stick spray to top to remove swirls.

Cool until firm. Remove fudge from pan by foil and cut into 1" square pieces.

Fruit Punch Fudge

This is a fun flavor, brightly colored and with an unexpected punch flavor too. It's a sure hit with both the young and the young at heart!

1/2 c. fruit punch mix (with sugar)
1 (12 oz.) bag white chocolate chips
1 (14 oz.) sweetened condensed milk
1 c. powdered sugar

Line 8" square pan with waxed paper.

In microwave safe bowl, heat milk just until steaming. Do not boil milk. Whisk in fruit punch mix. Stir in chocolate chips, and continue stirring until smooth and creamy. Beat in powdered sugar with a wooden spoon, stirring until mixture is smooth and cramy. (If it seems too thin, add a bit more powdered sugar.) Spread mixture into prepared pan. Refrigerate for 2-3 hours or until cold and firm. Remove from pan using waxed paper and cut into 1" squares. Store in air tight container in refrigerator for up to two weeks.

Cookie Dough Fudge

If you are a secret eater of cookie dough, you'll love this not so traditional fudge. Of course, even if you don't keep it a secret that you eat cookie dough, you'll still love it!

1/2 c. butter, softened
3/4 c. light brown sugar
1 tsp. vanilla extract
2 c. flour
1 (14 oz.) can sweetened condensed milk
1 c. mini chocolate chips
1/2 c. creamy peanut butter
1/3 c. white chocolate chips

In large bowl, mix butter and brown sugar until light and fluffy. Add vanilla and beat until combined. With mixer on low, alternate mixing in flour and sweetened condensed milk, mixing until combined. Gently fold in miniature chocolate chips with spatula.

Prepare 8" pan by lining with parchment paper, with extra over sides to make it easier to lift out fudge later. Press cookie dough into pan.

Cover bars with plastic wrap and refrigerate until firm, 3 hours or overnight.

Combine white chocolate chips and peanut butter in microwave safe bowl. Heat mixture in microwave in 15 second intervals until chocolate is beginning to melt, stirring after each interval. Stir mixture until smooth and creamy. Spread mixture over cookie dough mixture. Chill for 1 hour or until peanut butter mixture has set. Remove from pan and cut into 1" squares.

Store in refrigerator up to 1 week in air tight container.

Buttermilk Fudge

1 c. buttermilk
4 tbsp. butter
1 tbsp. corn syrup
2 c. sugar
1 tsp. baking soda
1/2 tsp. salt
1 tsp. vanilla
1 cup chopped, toasted pecans (optional)

Line an 8" square pan with foil and spray evenly with cooking spray.

Place buttermilk, butter, corn syrup, sugar, salt, and baking soda in a large pan over medium high heat. It will bubble a lot, so make sure the pan holds 3-4 times the amount of ingredients. Stir mixture until sugar and butter dissolves, then insert candy thermometer.

Continue cooking candy, stirring occasionally, until it reaches soft ball stage (240 degrees F.) Remove pan from heat, and pour on vanilla but do not stir. Allow candy to cool until it reaches about 150 degrees F. on the thermometer.

Add the chopped toasted nuts. Use a wooden spoon and stir candy until it thickens. When fudge becomes thick and starts to lose its gloss, quickly spread into prepared pan and smooth into a smooth layer.

Allow fudge to set at room temperature for 2 hours. Once set, remove from pan by using foil, and cut into 1" squares. Store fudge in air tight container at room temperature for up to two weeks.

Fantasy Fudge

Fantasy fudge is one of the classic recipes, and the term "fantasy" is often attached to any fudge recipe that uses marshmallow cream. They are considered "no-fail" recipes because they do not require precise cooking or long beating.

3 c. sugar
3/4 c. margarine
2/3 c. evaporated milk
1 (12 oz.) semi-sweet chocolate chips
1 (7 oz.) marshmallow cream
1 c. chopped walnuts
1 tsp. vanilla extract

Grease a 9x13" pan.

Mix sugar, margarine and evaporated milk in a large saucepan over medium heat, stirring to dissolve sugar. Bring mixture to a full boil for five minutes, stirring constantly.

Remove from heat. Stir in chocolate chips until melted and thoroughly combined. Beat in marshmallow cream, walnuts and vanilla. Transfer fudge to prepared pan and let cool before cutting into squares.

Double Chocolate Fudge

This is another version of fantasy or no-fail fudge. It's an easy recipe, using both cocoa and semi-sweet chocolate to achieve the double flavor.

1/4 c. butter, sliced
1 (12 oz.) evaporated milk
3 c. sugar
1 tsp. salt
1 (13 oz.) jar marshmallow cream
1 c. cocoa
24 oz. semi-sweet chocolate chips
1 tsp. vanilla
1 c. chopped walnuts or pecans (optional)

Prepare 9x13" pan by lining with foil and spraying with non-stick spray.

Combine butter, milk, sugar, salt, and marshmallow cream in large heavy saucepan. Stirring constantly, cook over medium heat until bubbly and smooth, about 12-14 minutes. Remove from heat.

Add cocoa, chocolate chips, and vanilla. Stir until melted. Stir in nuts. Pour into prepared pan and cool at room temperature.

Remove fudge from pan by lifting with foil. Peel away foil and cut into 1" pieces.

Store in airtight container for up to 2 weeks.

Penuche

4 c. brown sugar
1 1/2 c. milk
1 pinch salt
1/4 c. light corn syrup
3 tbsp. butter
1 tsp. vanilla

Line an 8" square pan with foil, and butter evenly or spray with nonstick spray.

In large 3 qt. saucepan, combine brown sugar, milk, corn syrup, and butter. Cook while stirring over medium heat until mixture comes to a boil. Then continue to cook, without stirring, cook to 240 degrees F. (soft ball stage).

Remove from heat. Cool to 120 degrees F. Add vanilla and beat until mixture starts to lose its gloss. Quickly pour into prepared pan.

Let sit at room temperature until firm (2-3 hours) and cut into 1" squares.

Dark Chocolate Fudge

1/2 c. light corn syrup
1/2 c. evaporated milk
2 pkg. (8 squares) semi-sweet baking chocolate
3/4 c. powdered sugar
2 tsp. vanilla extract
1 c. pecans (chopped)

Prepare 8" square pan by lining with foil, and either buttering it evenly or spraying with nonstick spray.

In large saucepan, mix together corn syrup and evaporated milk. Add chocolate and cook over medium-low heat, stirring constantly until chocolate melts. Remove from heat.

Stir in powdered sugar, vanilla extract and pecans. Beat with a large wooden spoon until thick and glossy. Quickly spread in prepared pan.

Refrigerate for 1-1/2 hours or until firm. Set out at room temperature for 20 minutes, cut into 1-inch squares.

Real Ginger Fudge

1 tbsp. butter
1 1/2 c. heavy whipping cream
3 c. sugar
1/4 c. light corn syrup
1/4 tsp. salt
3 tbsp. fresh grated ginger root

Prepare an 8" square pan by lining with foil and coating with butter or non-stick spray. Place butter into heat resistant mixing bowl and set aside.

Put cream, sugar, corn syrup, salt, and grated ginger into 3 quart saucepan. Cook over medium low heat, stirring constantly, until sugar has dissolved. (About ten minutes.) Raise heat to medium, and bring mixture to a boil. Wash sides of pan with a wet pastry brush to prevent crystals from forming in fudge. Attach pre-warmed candy thermometer to pan and continue to cook without stirring, until mixture reaches soft ball stage (240 degrees F.) This will take 10-15 minutes.

Immediately pour into mixing bowl with butter. Do not scrape out pan! Let mixture stand, undisturbed, until it registers 110 degrees, about 1-2 hours.

Remove thermometer from bowl. Using a sturdy wooden spoon, begin to gently stir mixture. Continue to stir, gradually beating faster, until mixture thickens, lightens in color, and begins to lose its shine. (4-5 minutes)

Pour into prepared pan, spreading evenly. Let cool at room temperature for about 1 hour, then cover with plastic and refrigerate until completely set, about 8 hours (or overnight.) Lift candy from pan by foil and cut into 1" squares.

Jalapeno Popper Fudge

This is “fussy" fudge, requiring some work before you even start making the fudge. Despite this, it is well worth the effort of making the candied jalapenos for the fudge.

In addition to the candied jalapenos, you will have a very spicy-hot flavored syrup that can be cooked further to the hard crack stage to create a hard candy for those who love hot candy--it will be very hot because most of the essential oils that create the "heat" of a chili pepper end up in the syrup, rather than in the candied jalapenos themselves.

With the green jalapenos and diced red pepper, it's great festive fudge, whether you are serving it at Christmas or for Cinco de Mayo!

1 c. thinly sliced fresh jalapenos
1 c. diced red bell pepper (or other red pepper)
3 c. sugar
1 c. water
1 (8 oz.) pkg. cream cheese
1/4 tsp. lemon flavor
1/2 tsp. vanilla
1/4 tsp. salt
1 (12 oz.) pkg. white chocolate chips, melted & cooled
3 c. sifted powdered sugar

Up to three days and at least three hours before making

fudge, candy peppers. Place sugar in large heavy saucepan. Add water and cook over medium high heat, stirring constantly, until sugar is completely dissolved and syrup is clear. Add peppers and cook without stirring for 15-20 minutes or until peppers become translucent. Using slotted spoon, remove peppers and lay in single layer on cookie sheet that has been lightly sprayed with nonstick spray. The more syrup that remains on peppers, the more heat they will retain, so for mild flavor, drain peppers very well! (A heat resistant tea strainer may also help drain peppers.) Let cool completely, and then place in airtight container or zip-close plastic bag in a cool, dry place until ready to use.

If desired, the remaining syrup can be used to make very hot candy. To do so, continue cooking syrup to hard crack stage (300 degrees F.) Pour candy onto lightly buttered cookie sheet or into prepared sucker molds. Do not give this candy to children--it can be VERY hot! When cool, break sheet of candy into pieces or remove suckers from molds. Candy can be colored with food coloring and additional flavor can be added with 1/2 tsp. of desired flavor.

Line 8" square pan with foil.

In bowl, beat cream cheese, lemon flavor, vanilla and salt until smooth. Beat in white chocolate. On medium low speed, add powdered sugar, 1 c. at a time. Increase speed to high and beat for 2 minutes. Fold in candied peppers by hand.

Spread mixture into prepared pan. Cover and refrigerate 8 hours or overnight. Turn fudge out onto work surface and carefully peel off foil. Turn fudge right side up and cut into 1" squares. Keep refrigerated and serve cold. Keeps up to a week in refrigerator when tightly wrapped.

Maple Bacon Fudge with sea salt

Here's another gourmet flavor of fudge, and easier than most because it uses marshmallows to ensure a creamy texture rather than complicated temperature and beating combination. Use your favorite bacon, cook the slices whole, drain them well on paper towels, and then chop coarsely, reserving some for the top of the fudge. Use a somewhat coarse sea salt to ensure that the grains of salt stand out with the bacon on top for the best visual impact.

2 c. brown sugar
1 c. evaporated milk
3 tbsp. butter
3 c. miniature marshmallows
3 c. white chocolate chips
2 lbs. bacon, cooked, drained, and chopped
2 1/2 tsp. maple extract

Prepare 9" pan by lining with foil and spraying with nonstick coating or buttering foil evenly.

In heavy saucepan, combine sugar, evaporated milk, and butter. Bring to a rolling boil over medium heat while stirring constantly. Keep at rolling boil for 5 minutes, without stirring. Remove from heat. Quickly stir in marshmallows, white chocolate, maple flavoring and all but 3/4 c. of bacon. Spread in prepared pan and sprinkle with sea salt and then with the reserved bacon pieces, pressing lightly to ensure bacon adheres to fudge. Chill in refrigerator 8 hours or overnight. Remove from pan by using foil and cut into 1" squares.

Store in refrigerator, in air tight container, for up to two weeks.

Cookies N Cream Fudge

The white fudge along with the crushed chocolate cookies creates the perfect fudge for all cookies and cream lovers, as well as a completely different appearance from other fudges.

3 c. sugar
3/4 c. butter
2/3 c. evaporated milk
2 c. white chocolate chips
½ c. miniature marshmallows
1 tsp. vanilla
1 1/2 c. coarsely crushed chocolate sandwich cookies (such as Oreos)

Prepare 9" square pan by lining with foil and spraying with nonstick spray.

In heavy saucepan, combine sugar, butter, and evaporated milk. Stirring constantly, bring to a boil over medium low heat. Continue stirring, and heat mixture to soft ball stage (240 degrees F.) (3-6 minutes) Remove from heat and stir in marshmallows and white chocolate chips until completely melted and smooth. Add vanilla and stir again to combine.

Gently fold in 1 c. cookie crumbles into fudge. Spread mixture into prepared pan and sprinkle remaining ½ cup of cookie crumbles on top, pressing lightly into fudge. Cool at room temperature until set. Remove fudge from pan using foil. Cut into 1" squares. Store fudge in air tight container for up to 2 weeks at room temperature.

ABOUT THE AUTHOR

Gia Scott was born, just like everyone else, but she also was born to a family that included politicians, used car dealers, and horse traders. Along with that illustrious lineage, she was related to vaudeville performers, horse trainers, cowboys, entrepreneurs, teachers, and preachers. With such diversity surrounding her from childhood, she still managed to grow up and develop a deep love of books. It was only natural that along the way, she would write them too. The Survivors: The Time of Chaos is her first published novel. More will undoubtedly follow. Freak Files: The Unexplained Tales is a collection of stories believed to be true to life.

After decades of experimental cooking, much to her family's chagrin (after all, the family is inflicted with the less-than-wonderful versions that never see print!) Gia began writing food articles and a food blog. It was inevitable that cookbooks would follow. This is the sixth cookbook. Previous titles include: All Chocolate—Easy & Economical Recipes Anyone Can Make At Home, 55 Fantastic Fudges, The All American Biscuit, 55 Frightfully Fun Foods, and A Home Style Thanksgiving.

Today, after many incarnations along the way, Gia Scott lives in Mississippi with her husband, three dogs, and two cats in a funny little house surrounded by very big and gnarly trees. Having reached that age of privilege, she can often be found in her garden, wearing peculiar clothes and tending her plants. When she can talk her husband into it, they enjoy going for road trips, looking for the elusive town of New Hope. In between road trips and gardening, she manages to fit in an internet radio talk show called the

Dawn of Shades, interviewing a variety of people, including other authors, and promoting causes dear to her heart.

In addition to all of that, she still maintains blogs on general topics, cooking & food, and camping, emergency preparedness & outdoors activities. She also helps with content for websites.

Links

Gia's other books can be found at http://bit/ly/GiaBooks

Gia's general blog is found at www.giascott.wordpress.com.

Gia's food blog is found at www.gulfcoastfoods.wordpress.com.

Gia's camping blog is found at www.getreadygo.wordpress.com.

Her website is found at www.exogenynetwork.com

Her author page on Facebook is found at www.facebook.com/giascottblogs

Made in the USA
San Bernardino, CA
16 August 2016